THE INVISIBLE BOND

Author: Gonzalo Estrada

While every precaution has been taken in the preparation of this book, the publisher assumes no responsibility for errors or omissions, or for damages resulting from the use of the information contained herein.

THE INVISIBLE BOND

First edition. October 10, 2024.

ISBN: 979-8227271938

Written by Gonzalo Estrada.

Table of Contents

Foreword

Since time immemorial, humans have shared their lives with animals. Dogs accompanied us on early hunts, cats watched over our homes, and so, almost naturally, our lives intertwined. Over time, that bond evolved. It was no longer just about companionship or utility; it became something deeper, an unbreakable emotional connection. And today, more than ever, pets are much more than life companions: they are members of our families, silent confidants, and an inexhaustible source of unconditional love.

This book, The Invisible Bond, was born from reflecting on that special connection we share with our pets. In a world that often overwhelms us with its speed and demands, our pets teach us to pause, to be present, to appreciate the little moments, and above all, to feel. With their silent loyalty and pure love, they have the power to transform us emotionally, to bring us comfort in difficult times, and to make us better people.

From the moment they look at us with those eyes that seem to see beyond what we can express, we know that something special has happened. They have chosen us, and we, without realizing it, have chosen them as well. In that first contact, that first caress or play, a bond begins to form that, though invisible to the eyes, is so strong and powerful that it transcends time.

Throughout this book, we will explore how this bond can not only improve our emotional lives but also that of our pets. We will see how our daily interactions, our routines, and our shared moments of calm can strengthen the relationship we have with them. We will learn to better understand their emotional needs and to respond with more empathy and love, recognizing that by taking care of them, we are also taking care of ourselves.

But this book is not just a guide on how to improve your relationship with your pet. It is a celebration of that unique and unrepeatable bond we share with them. It is an invitation to reflect on what it truly means to have a pet in our lives, on the value of their companionship, and on the lessons they teach us without uttering a single word.

In these pages, you will find touching stories, studies that reveal the emotional benefits of having a pet, and practical advice to make that bond even stronger. You will discover how your pet can be your greatest source of emotional support in times of stress, loneliness, or anxiety, and how you can return that love through small daily gestures.

In the end, the relationship between a human and their pet is not just a bond of care and coexistence. It is a deep and emotionally significant relationship that, when nurtured and valued, can transform our lives in ways we never imagined. This book is an invitation to cherish, care for, and deepen that relationship because in that connection, both humans and animals find an emotional refuge that helps us overcome any challenge and enjoy a fuller life.

I hope these pages not only inspire you to improve your relationship with your pet but also lead you to a greater understanding and appreciation of the incredible gift they offer us every day: pure, sincere, and selfless love.

Chapter 1: The Magic of the Human-Pet Bond

The connection between a human and their pet goes beyond words. It is a silent magic that happens when two beings, regardless of species, manage to communicate and understand each other from the heart. In this chapter, we will explore how that bond is formed, the factors that strengthen it, and how it can positively change the lives of both.

From the moment a pet enters our lives, a relationship is created that, over time, transforms into a constant source of joy and support. It is not just about care and responsibility; it is a genuine exchange of emotions and energy. As we get to know our four-legged companions, we begin to perceive their needs and feelings, and they, in turn, learn to read our emotional state and respond in ways that make us feel understood.

Science also supports this special connection. Studies have shown that physical contact with a pet can reduce cortisol levels, the stress hormone, and increase the production of oxytocin, known as the "love hormone." This physiological interaction not only improves our mood but also contributes to our physical and mental well-being.

But what makes some people feel such a deep connection with their pets, while others do not experience it as intensely? The answer lies in attention and commitment. Those who take the time to truly observe, play, and be present with their pets tend to experience a stronger and more meaningful bond. It is in the small daily gestures, such as petting your dog while watching TV or talking to your cat while preparing dinner, where the true power of the bond is found.

Throughout this chapter, we will hear moving stories of people who found unexpected emotional support in their pets, and how these relationships were crucial in overcoming difficult moments. We will also offer some practical guides on how to strengthen this connection, so you can experience a fulfilling and enriching life alongside your loyal companion.

Objective: To introduce the reader to the importance of emotional connection with pets and present key research on the positive impact of these relationships on mental health.

1. Introduction to the Human-Animal Bond

Explaining how and why pets have such a significant impact on our lives. Pets not only offer companionship but also contribute greatly to our physical and emotional well-being. Their presence can alleviate feelings of loneliness, give us a sense of purpose, and encourage healthy habits, like going for walks. Moreover, the simple act of petting a pet can trigger positive physiological responses, such as the release of oxytocin, which helps reduce stress and promote a sense of calm. Various scientific studies have shown that living with pets significantly reduces cortisol levels, the stress hormone, and can improve our overall mood and mental health. Psychological benefits include reduced stress, anxiety, and depression, as well as an overall improvement in mood and an increased sense of emotional security.

Various studies have shown the reduction of stress, anxiety, and depression in people who regularly interact with pets. A study by the University of Missouri found that petting a dog for just 15 minutes can reduce cortisol levels by 10%, while another study published in *Frontiers in Psychology* indicated that pet owners experience lower levels of anxiety and depression. Additionally, the American Heart Association has noted that having a pet, especially a dog, can help lower blood pressure and increase physical activity, which improves mood and overall well-being. These findings highlight how pets not only offer companionship but also provide tangible emotional support that enhances quality of life.

2. Oxytocin: The Happiness Hormone

Oxytocin, often known as the "happiness hormone" or the "love hormone," plays a fundamental role in creating and strengthening the bond between humans and pets. This hormone is released in large quantities during positive interactions, such as petting a pet, playing together, or simply spending quality time together. When we pet a dog or a cat, our body responds by releasing oxytocin, which induces an immediate sense of well-being and relaxation.

Research conducted by Azabu University in Japan has shown that prolonged eye contact between a dog and its owner can also increase oxytocin levels in both, creating a positive feedback loop that strengthens the emotional bond. This phenomenon is similar to what occurs between mothers and their babies, highlighting the depth of the connection we can have with our pets.

Another study published in *Hormones and Behavior* found that dog owners who spent more time interacting with their pets experienced higher levels of oxytocin compared to those who did not do so frequently. This hormone not only contributes to stress reduction but also plays a crucial role in improving trust and empathy in both humans and animals.

Additionally, oxytocin has a direct effect on lowering blood pressure and heart rate, contributing to a sense of calm and overall well-being. These physiological effects are key to understanding how the bond with a pet is not only emotional but also has tangible benefits for physical health. For example, petting a purring cat can be especially relaxing, increasing oxytocin levels and reducing stress.

In this sense, the release of oxytocin strengthens the bond by creating a sense of security and belonging, making both the human and the pet feel more connected and happier. These moments of daily connection are what truly build a solid relationship, based on mutual affection and deep understanding. Oxytocin, therefore, is an essential component in the human-animal relationship, helping to transform simple interactions into deeply meaningful experiences that improve the quality of life for both.

3. Mutual Emotional Interaction Between Humans and Pets

The relationship between humans and pets is not one-sided; both benefit emotionally from this special connection. Pets, like humans, experience emotions and can be affected by the quality of the bond with their owners. This constant and affectionate interaction generates mutual support that benefits both parties.

Pets, such as dogs and cats, develop a strong sense of belonging toward their owners, which provides them with a sense of security and well-being. Studies have shown that dogs, for example, produce oxytocin when they positively interact with humans, which not only strengthens the bond but also provides them with a sense of happiness and comfort. A study conducted by the University of Lincoln found that dogs living in environments where they receive constant attention and affection exhibit lower levels of anxiety and show more relaxed and balanced behaviors.

Additionally, cats also benefit from positive interaction with their owners. Although cats are commonly thought to be more independent, research has shown that they too develop secure attachments to their caregivers. A study by Oregon State University found that cats feel less stressed when they are near their owners and display attachment behaviors similar to those of dogs and human babies. This mutual closeness and affection create a safe and enriching environment for felines, resulting in more stable emotional well-being.

The emotional support pets receive from their owners also translates into improved physical health. Dogs, for example, are more willing to play, walk, and engage in activities when they perceive a strong emotional connection with their owners. This not only improves their physical condition but also contributes to their overall happiness. Cats, on the other hand, tend to purr more frequently when they are close to their humans, which is associated with a state of satisfaction and calm.

Throughout this chapter, we will see touching examples of how pets have shown loyalty and affection to their owners during difficult times, and how these gestures of love have been key to the recovery and emotional well-being of both. For example, during the COVID-19 pandemic, many people reported that their pets were a vital source of companionship and emotional support, while the animals also showed behaviors indicating a greater need for closeness and affection, demonstrating that the relationship was mutually supportive.

In summary, emotional interaction between humans and pets creates a reciprocal support relationship that benefits both emotional well-being and physical health. This deep connection is built day by day, through gestures of affection, care, and attention, which not only improve the quality of life of the human but also provide the pet with an environment filled with love, security, and happiness.

Chapter 2: Understanding Your Pet: The Emotional Language

Objective: Teach readers how to interpret their pets' emotional signals to improve communication and strengthen the bond.

1. Pet Body Language

A pet's body language is a fundamental tool for understanding their emotions and needs. Below, we describe key signals of emotions such as anxiety, stress, happiness, and relaxation, accompanied by practical examples to help owners better interpret what their pets are trying to communicate.

- Anxiety and Stress: Signs of anxiety and stress in dogs may include excessive panting, ears pulled back, a lowered or tucked tail, and a hunched posture. For example, if a dog is trembling, avoiding eye contact, and has its tail tucked, this is a clear sign that the dog is experiencing stress or anxiety. In cats, these emotions manifest through behaviors such as hiding, rapid tail movements, ears pulled back, or raised fur. A cat hiding under the bed or swishing its tail rapidly is likely feeling uncomfortable or stressed. These signals indicate that the pet needs a calmer environment or to feel safer.

- Happiness: Happiness is easy to recognize in dogs, as they often have a loose, wagging tail, a relaxed posture, and may stick out their tongue while showing a "smile." For example, a dog running toward you with its tail held high, wagging vigorously, and its mouth slightly open is expressing joy. Cats show happiness differently but just as clearly. They purr, rub against their owners, and often have their eyes half-closed. A cat that curls up next to you, purrs, and kneads with its paws is showing that it feels comfortable and happy.

- Relaxation: When a pet is relaxed, they display it through their body language. A relaxed dog may lie on its side or back, exposing its belly, and breathe calmly, indicating that it feels safe and comfortable. In cats, lying stretched out with paws forward or curling up with a relaxed body and closed eyes are clear signs of relaxation. For instance, a cat lying in the sun, fully stretched out, is signaling that it feels safe and relaxed in its environment.

- Interest or Curiosity: It's also important to identify when a pet is interested or curious about something. Dogs often tilt their heads to the side when they hear an unfamiliar sound or when something catches their attention. This gesture is a sign of curiosity and focus. Cats show their interest with upright ears and wide-open eyes, often accompanied by whiskers pushed forward. A cat fixating on a toy with ears forward is displaying curiosity and concentration.

Understanding your pet's body language is crucial to ensuring their well-being. It allows you to respond appropriately to their emotions, whether by offering comfort, giving them space, or simply acknowledging their happiness. These small daily interpretations strengthen the bond with your pets and promote a relationship built on understanding and respect.

2. Vocalizations and Typical Behaviors

Vocalizations and typical behaviors are a fundamental part of a pet's language and a key tool for owners to understand how their pets are feeling. Below, we explore the most common sounds in dogs and cats and how to interpret them to better understand your pet's emotional state.

- Dog Barking: Barking is one of the most common forms of communication for dogs, and its meaning can vary depending on tone, duration, and context. For example, a short, repetitive bark may indicate excitement or alertness, while a deep, prolonged bark may be a warning or sign of threat. A high-pitched, rapid bark accompanied by a relaxed posture and wagging tail may indicate joy or enthusiasm, especially when greeting you at home.

- Dog Howling: Howling is less common but often indicates loneliness or a need to communicate with other dogs. It can also be a response to certain high-pitched sounds, such as sirens. A dog that howls persistently while its owner is away may be experiencing separation anxiety.

- Dog Whining and Whimpering: Whining often indicates discomfort, fear, or a request for attention. For example, a dog whining near the door may be asking to go outside. Whimpering can also signal pain or discomfort, so it's important to pay attention to other physical signs if the whining persists.

- Cat Meowing: Cat meows can vary significantly, and each cat has its unique repertoire of sounds. A short, soft meow can be a greeting or a request for attention. Long, continuous meows may signal hunger or that the cat wants something specific, such as access to a room. A loud, prolonged meow can indicate discomfort or stress, especially if accompanied by tense body language.

- Cat Purring: Purring is, in most cases, a sign of satisfaction and relaxation. A cat that purrs while curled up in your lap feels safe and happy. However, cats can also purr when they are injured or ill as a form of self-soothing, so it's important to consider the context and other behaviors to accurately interpret the purring.

- Cat Hissing and Spitting: These sounds are clear signals of annoyance, fear, or threat. A hissing cat is indicating it needs space and feels threatened. Hissing is often accompanied by ears pulled back and a hunched posture, serving as a warning to stay away.

- Soft Barking and Growling in Dogs: Growling can have different meanings depending on the context. A soft growl during play may be a sign of fun, not necessarily aggression. However, a growl accompanied by a rigid posture and raised fur is a clear signal that the dog feels threatened or uncomfortable.

- Other Sounds: Cats can also make other sounds, such as chirps or trills, especially when they are excited or trying to get their owner's attention. These sounds are generally positive and indicate excitement or a friendly request for interaction. Dogs, on the other hand, may emit small snorts or sighs when relaxed or simply feeling comfortable.

Understanding these sounds and typical behaviors helps owners respond appropriately to their pets' emotional needs, ensuring a better relationship and strengthening the bond between human and animal. Continuous observation and practice allow owners to differentiate between a bark of alertness and one of happiness, or a meow for attention versus one of discomfort, thereby improving communication and empathy with their four-legged companions.

3. Strengthening Empathy with Your Pet

Strengthening empathy with our pets is essential to better understanding their needs and improving our relationship with them. Below are practical tips for being more aware of your pet's emotional needs, along with observation techniques and active listening that can help us improve empathy towards them.

- Observation Techniques: Observing your pet consciously is fundamental to recognizing their emotional states. Pay attention to their body language, vocalizations, and daily behaviors. For example, noticing when your dog is panting excessively or when your cat is hiding more than usual can be a sign of anxiety or stress. Keeping a mental or written record of these behaviors helps identify patterns and potential triggers, which is key to providing them with a safer and more comfortable environment.

- Active Listening: Active listening involves paying attention to the sounds your pets make and responding appropriately. When a dog barks insistently, instead of ignoring or immediately scolding them, try to understand what they are attempting to communicate. Are they excited, alert, or upset? Similarly, a cat that meows continuously may be trying to tell you they need something specific, like attention or food. Responding appropriately to these vocalizations helps your pet feel understood and cared for, strengthening the emotional connection.

- Recognizing and Responding to Emotions: Being empathetic with a pet also means recognizing and responding to their emotions. If your pet is showing signs of fear, such as hiding or trembling, it's important to give them space and not force interaction. Instead of trying to comfort them immediately, allow them to find a safe place where they can feel calm. Then, with gentleness and patience, try to comfort them. A dog that fears loud noises, such as fireworks, may benefit from a quiet, safe place to hide, accompanied by soft and calm words from their owner.

- Creating Consistent Routines: Pets feel more secure when they have a stable routine. Feeding them at the same time each day, going for regular walks, and establishing specific times for play help create a predictable and safe environment. This not only reduces stress but also reinforces trust between the pet and the owner. For example, a cat that knows when they will have playtime with their owner can anticipate it with joy, reducing anxious behavior.

- Physical Contact and Quality Time: Many pets need physical contact to feel connected to their owners. Slowly and steadily petting a dog can help reduce their anxiety and create a calm state. Cats, on the other hand, prefer contact in specific areas such as behind the ears or under the chin. Respecting their preferences and dedicating daily time for physical contact and play helps strengthen the emotional bond.

- Understanding Overstimulation Signs: Part of empathy involves recognizing when your pet needs space. For example, a dog that moves away after a while of petting is indicating that they've had enough, and it's important to respect that need. Cats are particularly clear when they feel overwhelmed: a sudden tail movement or a light bite are signs that they need to be left alone. Respecting these boundaries strengthens trust and shows your pet that their needs matter to you.

- Practical Examples: An example of how to strengthen empathy with your pet could be the following: if your dog shows anxiety every time you leave the house, try creating a calming ritual before your departure. Speak softly, pet them gently, and ensure they have an interactive toy to keep them entertained. This not only helps reduce the dog's anxiety but also reinforces the bond between you. Another example could be with a cat that tends to meow when they see you in the kitchen; instead of simply giving them food, take a moment to interact with them, talking to and

Chapter 3: Daily Routines to Strengthen the Bond

Objective: Provide practical exercises to improve the emotional relationship between humans and pets through daily activities.

1. The Power of Quality Time

Dedicating exclusive time to your pet is crucial for strengthening the bond, as it allows them to feel like an important part of your life. Just like humans, pets need attention and shared moments to establish a deep and meaningful connection. Below, we explain the importance of these moments and how you can make the most of the time spent with your animal companion.

- Sharing Quiet Moments: Quiet moments are essential for building a stable and deep relationship with your pet. Sitting together on the couch, gently and consistently petting your dog or cat, or simply relaxing side by side creates an atmosphere of peace and trust. These moments allow both owner and pet to relax and reduce stress levels. For example, cats often curl up next to their owners and purr, a clear sign of satisfaction and security. These moments of physical contact and tranquility generate an emotional connection that goes beyond words.

- Games and Dynamic Activities: In addition to quiet moments, play is an essential part of quality time. Playing with your pet not only provides them with physical exercise but also stimulates their minds and strengthens the relationship with their owner. Activities such as throwing a ball for your dog to fetch, using a laser pointer for your cat to chase, or even hide-and-seek games with treats are excellent ways to interact with your pet. These games not only promote fun but also teach them to collaborate and communicate with their owners. Be sure to choose activities that your pet enjoys and that stimulate them both mentally and physically.

- Daily Rituals: Creating and maintaining daily rituals is an excellent way to strengthen the bond with your pet. Routines provide security and stability, as animals are creatures of habit and feel more comfortable when they know what to expect. Establishing regular times for walking, feeding, and playing with your pet helps create a predictable environment that reduces stress and anxiety. For example, dedicating a few minutes each morning to brush your cat or take your dog for a walk before starting the day are rituals that not only improve your pet's quality of life but also reinforce the emotional bond between you.

- Outdoor Time: Walks and time outdoors are valuable opportunities to share with your pet. Dogs, in particular, enjoy these moments, as they allow them to explore their surroundings, exercise, and spend time with you. To make walks a bonding experience, avoid distractions like your phone and focus on the shared experience. Observe how your dog explores, speak to them in a soft, positive tone, and allow them to enjoy the smells and sounds of their environment. This conscious presence during the walk benefits not only your pet but also helps you disconnect from daily stress and enjoy the present moment.

In conclusion, quality time is the key to building a strong and meaningful relationship with your pet. Whether through moments of calm, active play, daily rituals, or mindful walks, each shared moment contributes to strengthening the bond and ensuring the emotional well-being of both. Let's remember that our pets depend on us not only for their physical needs but also for affection and connection.

2. Mental and Emotional Stimulation Exercises

Mental and emotional stimulation is essential for the well-being of our pets, as it provides enrichment beyond physical activity. Below are several activities that will not only keep your pet busy but also help strengthen the emotional connection between you:

- Hide-and-Seek Games: This activity stimulates both the body and mind of the pet. You can hide treats or toys in different areas of the house and encourage your pet to find them. This not only activates their sense of smell but also provides a mental challenge that keeps them engaged and entertained. Additionally, the moment of celebration when they find the object reinforces the bond between owner and pet.

- Interactive Toys: Interactive toys, such as treat dispensers or puzzles for dogs and cats, are excellent for keeping your pet mentally stimulated. These toys encourage critical thinking and help combat boredom, which can lead to unwanted behaviors. Moreover, toys that require owner participation, such as automatic ball launchers, offer opportunities to directly interact with your pet and strengthen the emotional bond.

- Training and Learning New Tricks: Dedicating time each day to teaching your pet new tricks is an excellent way to keep them mentally stimulated. It not only challenges them intellectually but also improves communication and trust between you and your pet. For example, teaching a dog to shake hands, spin, or fetch objects not only keeps them focused but also fosters cooperation. In the case of cats, tricks like sitting or jumping through a hoop can be equally entertaining and rewarding.

- Challenging Play Sessions: Introducing elements that challenge your pet's mind during play is another way to offer stimulation. For example, using cardboard boxes to create mazes or hiding toys inside them helps the pet think and explore. This type of activity is ideal for both cats and dogs, as it allows them to exercise their natural instincts for exploration and problem-solving.

- Sensory Toys and Quality Time: Toys that stimulate different senses, such as those that make noise or have various textures, are also useful for providing mental and emotional stimulation. For instance, cats often enjoy toys that mimic the sound of small prey, while dogs can benefit from toys that crunch or have rough surfaces. By introducing variety in the toys, you ensure that the experience is interesting and rewarding for your pet.

- Relaxation and Mindfulness Exercises: Besides active mental stimulation, it is also important to help our pets relax. Exercises such as teaching your dog to wait patiently before receiving a treat or practicing "stay" are excellent ways to encourage calmness and self-control. These exercises not only improve obedience but also provide a sense of accomplishment and satisfaction for both owner and pet.

These daily activities not only enrich your pet's life but also allow you to spend quality time with them, contributing to the emotional well-being of both. By keeping your pet mentally stimulated, you prevent boredom and foster a happier, more balanced life.

3. Mindful Walks: A Shared Emotional Experience

Walks are much more than an opportunity for pets to exercise; they are a key moment to strengthen the bond between owner and pet. To make walks a truly shared emotional experience, it is essential to be present and take advantage of the outdoor time mindfully. Below are some strategies for making each walk a meaningful moment:

- Be Present and Avoid Distractions: During walks, it is important to avoid distractions such as using your phone. Being present means focusing on the pet and the environment you share. Observe how your dog explores, enjoys the smells, and pay attention to their body language. Speaking to them in a soft, positive tone reinforces the connection and lets them know that you are sharing that moment with them. Mindful presence not only strengthens the bond but also contributes to mutual calm and enjoyment.

- Encourage Exploration: Walks are an opportunity for your pet to explore and discover their surroundings. Allow your dog to take the time to sniff and observe their environment. Exploration mentally stimulates the pet, as it allows them to exercise their natural instinct for investigation. Instead of rushing the walk, let your pet set the pace and explore in their own way, which generates a sense of freedom and satisfaction. Cats walking with a harness can also benefit from this opportunity to explore, as long as the environment is safe.

- Incorporate Games and Activities: Walks can also include games that strengthen the emotional connection. You can bring a ball to throw for your dog to fetch or practice obedience exercises like "stay" or "come." These activities not only promote physical exercise but also reinforce communication and trust between you. Each time your pet responds positively to a command during the walk, the bond of cooperation and trust is strengthened.

- Enjoy the Natural Environment: Take advantage of the outdoors by enjoying the natural environment. Walks in parks, trails, or green areas offer visual and olfactory stimuli for both the pet and the owner. Take a moment to appreciate the scenery, nature, and the present moment. This is beneficial not only for the pet but also for the owner, as it reduces stress and improves the emotional well-being of both.

- Create Predictable Walking Routines: Pets like consistency, and having a regular walking schedule can help reduce anxiety and increase positive anticipation. If your pet knows that every day there will be a specific time for a walk, this creates a sense of security and reinforces the bond. Additionally, these regular walks are an opportunity to develop a non-verbal language between owner and pet, creating an intuitive connection based on mutual understanding.

- Connect on an Emotional Level: Use the walk as an opportunity to connect emotionally with your pet. Talking to them, petting them when they stop, or taking breaks to give them a treat reinforces affection and mutual understanding. These gestures show that the walk is not just an obligation but a moment of connection and shared enjoyment. The emotional connection is strengthened when the pet perceives that their owner is engaged and enjoying the moment as much as they are.

In conclusion, mindful walks are a powerful tool for strengthening the bond with your pet. Being present, encouraging exploration, including games, and enjoying the environment together are strategies that turn each walk into an enriching experience for both. By making walks a special moment, you will create positive memories and reinforce the relationship with your animal companion.

Chapter 4: Mutual Emotional Support: How Your Pet Helps You Overcome Challenges

Chapter Summary: This chapter explores how pets act as sources of emotional support during moments of crisis or difficulty. Through touching stories, scientific studies, and practical techniques, readers will discover how their relationship with their pets can be a key tool in coping with stress, anxiety, and grief. Pets not only offer companionship, but they can also be genuine emotional pillars, helping their owners find strength in dark times.

1. Heartwarming Stories of Emotional Support

Objective: Inspire readers through real testimonies illustrating how pets provide emotional support to their owners
during difficult situations.

Personal stories have a unique power to emotionally connect with readers. In this section, you can present accounts of people who have experienced the comfort and companionship of their pets during times of distress.

Example 1: Comfort After a Loss

Imagine Marta, who, after losing her mother, found herself in deep sadness. Emotionally isolated, she found it difficult to continue with her daily routines. However, her dog Max, a loyal German Shepherd, seemed to sense her pain. Every time Marta cried, Max would approach and place his head on her lap, offering silent but powerful comfort. Through these small daily interactions, Marta began to reconnect with the world, regaining her emotional stability.

Example 2: Overcoming Anxiety with a Furry Companion

Juan had always struggled with anxiety, but after an especially intense episode, he decided to adopt Luna, a shelter cat. Luna seemed to have a sixth sense for detecting when Juan was on the verge of a panic attack. Without needing words, Luna would curl up next to him, purring softly, which helped Juan calm his breathing and find his emotional center. Thanks to Luna's constant presence, Juan learned to better manage his anxiety.

Commentary: These stories not only touch the heart but also demonstrate the tangible impact of animal companionship on people's lives, showing how pets can help their owners find comfort and emotional strength.

2. Pets and Emotional Resilience

Objective: Explain how having a pet can strengthen an owner's emotional resilience, helping them overcome difficult times.

Emotional resilience is the ability to recover quickly from challenging situations, and pets play a key role in developing this skill in their owners.

a) Routines that Provide Stability

One of the most important aspects of having a pet is the routine that their care requires. Feeding, walking, or simply attending to the basic needs of a pet demands regularity, which can bring structure and meaning to the life of a person going through an emotionally difficult time. This daily commitment can act as an anchor, providing a sense of purpose and helping people stay active and focused, even in the darkest moments.

b) Responsibility as a Source of Resilience

Having the responsibility of caring for a pet also fosters emotional resilience. Instead of focusing solely on their pain, a pet owner learns to care about the well-being of another living being. This responsibility can drive faster emotional recovery, as it forces the person to stay present and fulfill their pet's needs, which in many cases has a positive effect on their own emotional stability.

c) Positive Interactions that Lift the Spirit

Pets are experts at bringing moments of unexpected joy. Whether it's a cat chasing a string or a dog excited by a simple walk, these small moments of fun and emotional connection can help owners relieve stress and refocus on the positive aspects of life. These small emotional "breathers" are essential for building resilience.

3. Emotional Therapy with Pets

Objective: Describe the impact of pets in emotional treatments and how they are being used in assisted therapies to improve mental well-being.

Animal-assisted therapies have gained popularity as an effective complement for treating emotional disorders such as anxiety, post-traumatic stress disorder (PTSD), and depression.

a) The Science Behind Pet Therapy

Studies have shown that interactions with animals, such as petting a dog or cat, can lower cortisol levels (the stress hormone) and increase oxytocin levels. These effects have a direct impact on reducing stress and anxiety. Animals also promote greater production of serotonin and dopamine, neurotransmitters associated with feelings of happiness and well-being.

b) Success Stories in Emotional Therapy

In clinical settings, pets have proven useful in treating patients with severe emotional issues. For example, therapy dogs have helped reduce anxiety symptoms in veterans suffering from PTSD, providing them with a constant source of comfort and calm. Similarly, in hospitals or nursing homes, therapy animals have helped the elderly find comfort and reduce feelings of loneliness and depression.

c) Animal-Assisted Therapies: A Growing Tool

This section can discuss how animal-assisted therapy is not limited to dogs and cats. Horses, rabbits, and other animals have been used in various types of therapies. These programs aim to foster the development of emotional skills such as empathy, responsibility, and self-control. The presence of an animal can reduce the perception of judgment, allowing patients to open up more easily and, in many cases, address deeper emotional traumas.

4. The Unconditional Bond: A Refuge in Times of Adversity

Objective: Reflect on the unconditional value of pets and how this unique relationship can be a source of emotional security for their owners.

One of the most significant aspects of the human-pet relationship is the unconditional love that pets provide. Unlike human relationships, which can be complex and sometimes difficult, pets do not judge or impose expectations. They are there in both good and bad times, offering a calming and stable presence.

a) Loyalty and Constant Support

This section can highlight the value of having a loyal and constant presence, especially in times of adversity. Facing emotional challenges can be a lonely experience, but pets offer unconditional companionship, which reduces the feeling of isolation.

b) Reducing Stress in Crisis Situations

This section can explore how simply having a pet can help reduce emotional stress in crisis situations. From the release of endorphins when petting an animal to the silent comfort they offer, pets act as natural buffers against stress.

Chapter Conclusion: Mutual Emotional Support at Its Best

Think in on how the emotional bond between humans and pets can be a true source of strength and support during the hardest times in life. This bond not only benefits the owners but also offers pets a fulfilling emotional life, creating a relationship where both support each other. you should feel inspired to value their relationship with their pets even more and to recognize that, in the toughest moments, they are never alone—they always have their unconditional companion by their side.

Chapter 5: Joint Relaxation Techniques: Mindfulness for You and Your Pet

Chapter Summary: This chapter introduces readers to the world of mindfulness and relaxation techniques that both pet owners and their pets can practice together. In an increasingly fast-paced and stressful world, learning to relax with our pets not only improves our mental health but also strengthens the emotional bond. Through practical and simple exercises, this chapter teaches how to integrate mindfulness practices, therapeutic massages, and relaxation routines to create a shared wellness experience.

1. Meditation with Pets: Connecting Through Calm

Objective: Teach how to practice meditation and mindfulness techniques with their pets, creating moments of shared tranquility.

Meditation is not only beneficial for humans; pets can also experience the calming effects of a relaxed and serene environment. Practicing mindfulness with a pet creates a space of deep connection, where both can relax and emotionally synchronize.

a) Introduction to Mindfulness with Your Pet

Mindfulness is about being present in the moment, observing thoughts and sensations without judgment. Involving your pet in this practice means paying attention to how they respond to their surroundings, observing their body language, breathing, and how they synchronize with your calmness.

b) Joint Breathing Exercise

simple exercise: sit next to your pet in a quiet space. Observe their breathing and try to sync your own breath with theirs. Breathe deeply and slowly, allowing your calmness to influence your pet's energy. This exercise can last between 5 to 10 minutes and is ideal for creating a shared atmosphere of calm.

c) Guided Meditation with Your Pet

Do a meditation focus on the presence of their pet, noticing how their body feels nearby, how they breathe, and their subtle movements. This helps center the mind, release tension, and strengthen the emotional connection. Throughout the meditation, the reader can observe how the calm they feel is reflected in their pet's relaxed behavior.

2. Therapeutic Massages: Physical and Emotional Relaxation

Objective: learn simple and safe massage techniques to relax both the pet and the owner, promoting a state of mutual calm and well-being.

Physical contact is a powerful way to create an emotional connection and reduce stress, both in humans and animals. Through therapeutic massage, it is possible not only to relieve physical tension but also to foster greater intimacy and trust between the owner and their pet.

a) Benefits of Massage for Pets and Their Owners

Massage can help pets reduce anxiety, improve blood circulation, and relieve muscle tension. Likewise, owners can experience a calming effect by focusing on the slow, rhythmic movements of the massage, which encourages presence and attunement to their pet's physical needs.

b) Simple Massage Techniques

Try easy-to-perform massage techniques at home, such as:

- Neck and Shoulder Massage: Start by gently stroking your pet's neck and shoulders, using slow circular motions with your fingertips. This type of massage is ideal for releasing tension in areas where pets tend to accumulate stress, especially after a busy day.

- Relaxing Back Massage: Place your palms on either side of your pet's spine and gently move them downward, following the length of the spine. This type of contact not only helps relax back muscles but also creates a sense of comfort and security.

- Paw Massage: Pets' paws can also accumulate tension, especially after long walks. Gently stroking and massaging the paws can be very relaxing, especially if done after a walk or physical activity.

c) The Power of Conscious Touch

massage should not be rushed but rather practiced consciously. While massaging your pet, focus on how their body responds, adjusting pressure and movements as needed. The goal is to create a relaxing experience for both, paying attention to your pet's breathing rhythm and any signs of comfort or discomfort.

3. Bedtime Relaxation Routines

Objective: Create a nighttime routine that helps both the owner and the pet prepare for a restful sleep, establishing a mutual calm ritual before bed.

A bedtime relaxation routine not only promotes better sleep but also strengthens the emotional bond with your pet at the end of the day. The focus here is on creating a serene environment that benefits both, using moments of calm to reduce accumulated stress and anxiety.

a) The Importance of a Bedtime Routine

Pets, like humans, thrive on consistency. An established bedtime routine can signal to your pet that it's time to relax and prepare for sleep. This habit, when practiced together, reinforces a sense of security and tranquility for both.

b) Quiet Moments Before Bed

Try a simple relaxation ritual, such as dimming the lights, playing soft music, and sitting with your pet in a quiet space. Take a few minutes to pet your pet in silence, focusing on the gentle movements of your hands and slow, deep breathing. This process will not only help your pet relax but can also calm your mind and body before sleep.

c) Quiet Reading and Company

For owners who enjoy reading before bed, they can include their pets in this routine. By reading in a soft, calm voice while your pet snuggles beside you, you create a serene atmosphere that both can enjoy. This type of activity can be particularly relaxing for cats, who often feel more comfortable in a quiet, low-activity environment.

d) Final Care Routine

Including simple actions like gently brushing your pet or giving them a final pat can be a relaxing way to end the day. This type of care not only prepares the pet for a good night's sleep but also creates a feeling of mutual affection and well-being.

4. Emotional Synchronization Through Shared Rest

Objective: See how the act of resting together can enhance emotional synchronization between the owner and their pet, strengthening the bond through moments of shared calm and comfort.

Rest is a time when emotions and bodies naturally synchronize. Pets often adapt to their owner's emotional rhythm, and vice versa. This creates an ideal opportunity to deepen the connection between both.

a) The Value of Shared Rest

Watch how the simple act of resting next to your pet, whether on the couch, bed, or a cozy corner, can have a positive emotional impact. Physical proximity and shared relaxation reinforce the sense of security for both the pet and the owner.

b) Creating a Restful Atmosphere

Suggest ways to create a cozy space to rest together, such as using soft blankets, cushions, or pet beds. Relaxing scents like lavender or chamomile can help establish a calming atmosphere. By creating an environment of tranquility, both you and your pet can enjoy a greater sense of well-being.

Chapter Conclusion: Cultivating Emotional Well-Being Together

Let's conclude the chapter by reflecting on how joint relaxation practices not only reduce stress and improve physical well-being but also create a deeper emotional connection. Mindfulness techniques, massages, and nighttime routines establish a foundation of trust and mutual care that benefits both humans and pets. By cultivating these moments of calm, owners and pets can enjoy a more emotionally balanced and connected life.

Chapter 6: Strengthening the Emotional Bond in the Long Term

Chapter Summary: This chapter delves into the keys to maintaining a solid and emotionally healthy relationship with pets over the years. It explores how consistency, adapting to different stages of a pet's life, and creating meaningful rituals can strengthen the emotional bond in the long term. Beyond daily moments, a practical guide is offered to ensure that, over time, the relationship not only endures but also enriches and evolves.

1. Emotional Consistency: The Pillar of a Long-Term Bond

Objective: Let's Highlight the importance of consistency in attention, affection, and time spent with pets to maintain a strong emotional bond. Emotional consistency is key to any relationship, and this is especially true in the relationship with our pets. Over the years, animals rely on regular routines and behaviors to feel secure and connected with their owners.

a) The Impact of Routine on Emotional Well-Being

Pets thrive on predictability. Having set schedules for feeding, walks, playtime, and relaxation gives them a sense of security and stability. For dogs, knowing they will have their daily walk at a specific time or receive attention at key moments of the day can reduce stress and anxiety. For cats, having designated moments of play or companionship is also essential for their emotional well-being.

b) Consistency in Affection: Building Lasting Trust

Like humans, pets need to feel that their relationship with their owner is secure and stable. Being consistent with displays of affection—such as petting, soft words, and quality time—ensures that pets feel loved and valued. This consistency reinforces mutual trust and respect, facilitating a deeper and more fulfilling relationship.

c) Maintaining the Emotional Connection During Times of Change

It's normal for owners to face changes in their routines due to new jobs, moves, or personal situations. During these periods, it is crucial to make a conscious effort to maintain the emotional connection with the pet. Even though circumstances change, dedicating exclusive time to your pet, even in small moments, ensures that the relationship remains a priority and that the pet does not feel emotionally neglected.

2. Adapting to Different Stages of Your Pet's Life

Objective: Teach owners how to adjust their care and emotional approach based on their pet's age and changing needs.

As pets age, their physical, emotional, and cognitive needs change. It is important for owners to adapt how they interact with and care for their animals at each life stage, from the exuberant energy of youth to the calm and special care required in old age.

a) Puppies and Kittens: Establishing the Bond's Foundation

In the early stages of life, puppies and kittens are full of energy and curiosity, making it a key time to establish a strong bond. Time spent playing, early training, and socialization not only help them develop physically and mentally but also reinforce the emotional connection with their owner.

- The Value of Positive Training: Using positive reinforcement, such as treats and praise, during training strengthens trust and the relationship. These early interactions set the tone for a relationship based on mutual respect and affection.

- Caring for Their Emotional Development: Puppies and kittens are emotionally vulnerable at this stage, and it is important that they feel safe and cared for so they grow into well-balanced adults.

b) Adulthood: Maintaining a Strong Relationship

When pets reach adulthood, they leave behind the frantic energy of youth but still enjoy active interaction with their owners. It is crucial to continue dedicating quality time to the pet, ensuring that both play and exercise remain part of the daily routine.

- Activities That Strengthen the Bond: At this age, pets enjoy more structured activities such as long walks, games of fetch, or even advanced training. These shared experiences strengthen the bond and keep the pet mentally and emotionally active.

- The Importance of Variety in Routine: While consistency is key, introducing new activities, such as new toys or walks in different locations, helps keep the pet stimulated and avoids monotony.

c) Old Age: Special Care and Attention

As pets age, their bodies and minds change, and it is crucial to adjust care to meet their new needs. In this stage, the emotional connection deepens as owners become more aware of their pet's fragility and seek to make their old age peaceful and happy.

- Adapted Physical Care: Older pets may require changes in diet, less exercise, or more frequent veterinary visits. Ensuring they are comfortable and free from pain is essential for their emotional well-being.

- Strengthening the Bond in Calm Moments: Older pets enjoy tranquility. Establishing calm moments together, such as cuddling or simply being in the same space, reinforces the emotional connection. In this stage, gentle physical contact and kind words are powerful ways to continue showing affection.

3. Rituals to Strengthen the Connection Over Time

Objective: Provide ideas for small daily or weekly rituals that can help reinforce the emotional bond between owner and pet over the years.

Shared rituals not only provide structure but also create lasting memories and moments of deep connection. When performed regularly, these rituals help strengthen the emotional bond, allowing both the owner and the pet to anticipate and enjoy these special moments.

a) Daily Rituals of Emotional Connection

Small daily routines, though they may seem insignificant, can have a big impact on the relationship between owner and pet.

- The Daily Greeting: Take advantage of the moment when you come home to have a special greeting with your pet. Spend a few minutes petting them, talking softly, and giving them your full attention to reinforce the emotional bond and give your pet a sense of belonging and security.

- Pre-Bedtime Play: Creating a small ritual of play or relaxation before bed can be a valuable time for connection. Something as simple as a few minutes of light play with a favorite toy or a session of petting can help end the day on a positive emotional note.

b) Weekly Quality Time Rituals

In addition to daily interactions, planning more structured weekly activities can further strengthen the bond.

- Special Outings: Dedicate one day a week to taking your dog to a new park or spending quality time outdoors. For cats, setting aside one day a week for interactive play with toys or mental enrichment exercises can be a fun way to strengthen the relationship.

- Weekly Grooming Session: Many animals enjoy physical care, such as brushing or grooming. Setting aside time each week to care for your pet's appearance not only improves their health but also offers an opportunity for close and affectionate contact.

c) Celebrating Milestones

Don't forget to celebrate special moments with your pet, such as their birthday or the anniversary of their adoption. Preparing a special meal, organizing a day of activities, or simply spending extra time with them on these occasions reminds both of you of the importance of the relationship and creates lasting memories.

4. The Power of Long-Term Commitment

Objective: Reflect on the importance of the emotional and practical commitment involved in caring for a pet throughout their life, and how this commitment can enrich both the owner's and the pet's life.

Commitment to a pet is not just a practical responsibility but also an emotional one. Maintaining the emotional bond requires dedication, but the reward is a deep and fulfilling relationship that enriches both lives.

a) The Importance of Staying Present

As time goes on, it can be easy to take the relationship with our pet for granted. However, it is crucial to remember that, just like in any relationship, it is necessary to keep investing time, attention, and affection. Staying present in your pet's emotional life ensures that the bond continues to grow, even after many years.

b) Facing Challenges Together

Certain phases of a pet's life may present challenges, such as health issues or behavioral changes. Maintaining commitment during these difficult times strengthens the relationship and shows your pet that you will stand by their side, no matter the difficulties.

c) The Lesson of Loyalty and Unconditional Love

Pets teach us important lessons about unconditional love and loyalty. This chapter can conclude by highlighting how, by being consistent and dedicated in our relationship with them, we can learn and apply these lessons in other areas of our lives.

Chapter Conclusion: The Legacy of an Emotionally Fulfilling Relationship

End The chapter by reflecting on how, over time, the relationship with a pet not only improves our emotional life but also leaves a legacy of love, commitment, and deep connection. You should feel that, by dedicating time and effort to maintaining and nurturing the bond with your pet, will be building a relationship that will last a lifetime and enrich them in ways they never imagined at the beginning.

Chapter 7: Your Pet's Physical and Emotional Health: A Holistic Approach

Chapter Summary: This chapter explores the connection between physical health and emotional well-being in pets, demonstrating how a holistic approach is key to their overall wellness. Good nutrition, regular exercise, and veterinary care not only affect their bodies but also their emotional state and behavior. By understanding how these elements work together, owners can provide complete care that benefits both the physical health and emotional balance of their furry companions.

1. Nutrition and Its Impact on Emotional Well-Being

Objective: Explain how a balanced diet is essential not only for physical health but also for the pet's emotional state.

Nutrition is one of the fundamental pillars of a pet's well-being. A proper diet not only keeps the pet in good physical condition but also impacts their behavior, energy levels, and emotional state. Nutritional deficiencies can lead to problems such as irritability, fatigue, and even depression in some animals.

a) Benefits of a Balanced Diet

A balanced diet helps regulate energy levels and improves a pet's mood. When a pet receives the right nutrients, such as quality proteins, healthy fats, and vitamins, their body functions optimally, positively influencing their emotional well-being.

- Proteins and Essential Amino Acids: Consuming quality proteins is essential for producing neurotransmitters like serotonin, which helps regulate mood. Amino acid deficiencies can contribute to anxiety and aggression in some pets.

- Healthy Fats: Omega-3 and Omega-6 fatty acids, found in fish and vegetable oils, are vital for brain and nervous system health, which influences the emotional stability of pets.

b) Foods That Promote Emotional Well-Being

Some foods, in addition to being nutritious, can have a positive impact on a pet's behavior. For example, antioxidant-rich foods like fruits and vegetables can boost the immune system, which also helps maintain a more relaxed and balanced attitude.

- Natural Supplements: Certain supplements, such as glucosamine for joints or fish oil for skin and brain health, not only improve physical health but can also have a calming effect and enhance a pet's general behavior.

c) Emotional Consequences of Poor Nutrition

An unbalanced diet can cause emotional problems such as irritability or apathy. Overweight or obese pets, for example, not only face physical health risks but also experience low self-esteem and altered behavior, becoming less active and more prone to depression or stress.

2. Exercise and Its Role in Mental Health

Objective: Regular physical exercise is essential not only for a pet's physical health but also for reducing stress, anxiety, and promoting a healthy emotional state.

Exercise is crucial for both the physical health and emotional stability of pets. Animals that don't get enough physical activity may become bored, anxious, or even destructive. On the other hand, those that engage in regular exercise experience lower stress levels, are calmer, and have more balanced behaviors.

a) Emotional Benefits of Regular Exercise

Exercise releases endorphins, neurotransmitters associated with feelings of happiness and well-being. It also helps release excess energy that, if not properly channeled, can lead to anxious or aggressive behaviors.

- Dogs: Daily walks and active games like fetch not only keep dogs fit but also help them relax and remain emotionally balanced. Dogs that don't get enough exercise may become restless, bark excessively, or even display destructive behavior.

- Cats: While cats don't need the same level of exercise as dogs, they still require physical stimulation. Playing with toys that simulate hunting, such as fishing rods or lasers, allows them to release energy and keep their minds active, reducing boredom and anxiety.

b) Activities Adapted to Age and Physical Condition

It's important to tailor exercise to the pet's energy level, breed, and age. Puppies and young dogs will need more physical activity to burn energy, while older dogs may require shorter, gentler walks. For cats, some will enjoy chasing games, while others prefer calmer activities like interactive toys.

c) How Exercise Reduces Anxiety and Stress

Lack of exercise can increase anxiety and stress levels in pets. Regular physical activities help regulate sleep cycles, reduce destructive behavior related to separation anxiety, and improve overall mood.

3. Regular Veterinary Checkups: The Key to Detecting Physical and Emotional Issues

Objective: Emphasize the importance of regular veterinary checkups to detect health problems that may influence a pet's emotional well-being.

Regular checkups are essential not only for detecting physical health issues but also for identifying early signs of emotional or behavioral problems. An undetected health issue can cause changes in a pet's behavior and emotional state, often misinterpreted as "bad behavior" when it is actually a sign of physical discomfort.

a) Early Detection of Emotional Issues

During veterinary checkups, the vet can observe behavioral changes that may indicate a health or emotional problem. For example, loss of appetite, lethargy, or sudden aggression could be symptoms of an underlying illness.

- Dental or Joint Problems: Pain caused by dental or joint problems can make a pet irritable or reluctant to socialize.

- Chronic Diseases and Their Emotional Impact: Conditions like arthritis, kidney disease, or heart problems can affect a pet's behavior, making them less active and more prone to depression or anxiety.

b) Vaccinations, Deworming, and Disease Prevention

Keeping pets up to date with vaccinations and deworming is also crucial for their emotional well-being. Pets suffering from internal or external parasites, for example, may experience constant discomfort, affecting their mood and behavior.

c) Emotional and Behavioral Checkups

Some specialized vets also offer emotional and behavioral evaluations, where they can suggest changes in diet, environment, or activity levels to improve the pet's overall well-being. These evaluations can be especially helpful if the pet has shown recent or unexplained behavioral changes.

4. Preventing Stress During Veterinary Visits

Objective: Provide strategies to make veterinary visits less stressful for pets, reducing the negative impact on their emotional well-being.

For many pets, visits to the vet can be a stressful experience. However, with the right techniques, it is possible to minimize the fear and anxiety associated with these visits.

a) Gradual Desensitization to the Vet

If veterinary visits are a significant source of stress, owners can work on gradually desensitizing their pet to the clinic. This involves taking the pet to the clinic just to greet the staff or receive treats, without undergoing procedures, so they associate the place with positive experiences.

b) Creating a Positive Experience Before and After the Visit

Ensure that the trip to the vet is as relaxed as possible. Bringing the pet's favorite toys or blankets can help create a sense of security. After the visit, offering a reward or spending time playing can help the pet associate the experience with something positive.

c) Calming Products and Relaxation Techniques

For particularly anxious pets, calming products such as pheromones or natural supplements can be used before the vet visit. Additionally, speaking in a calm tone and giving gentle strokes during the visit can help soothe the pet's nerves.

Chapter 8: Adopting a Pet: The Beginning of an Emotional Bond

Chapter Summary: Adopting a pet is an act that transforms not only the animal's life but also the owner's. This chapter guides readers through the adoption process, offering practical advice on how to choose the right pet for their home and how to prepare emotionally and physically to welcome a new companion. Additionally, it delves into how to establish a strong emotional bond from the very beginning, ensuring that both the owner and the pet can adjust to their new life together in harmony.

1. How to Choose the Right Pet for You: Factors to Consider

Objective: Help readers reflect on the key factors to consider when choosing a pet, ensuring it aligns with their lifestyle and expectations.

Adopting a pet is an important decision that requires careful thought. Not all pets are suitable for every person or lifestyle. This section focuses on helping prospective owners make responsible choices.

a) Lifestyle and available time:

The first factor readers should consider is their lifestyle. Some pets require more time and attention than others, and it's essential for the owner to ensure they can provide the necessary care.

- Active dogs vs. calm dogs: If you lead an active lifestyle and enjoy outdoor activities, a high-energy dog like a Border Collie or Labrador Retriever might be suitable. On the other hand, if you prefer a more relaxed lifestyle, breeds like the French Bulldog or Basset Hound might be a better fit.

- Cats and their levels of independence: In general, cats are more independent than dogs, making them more suitable for people who have less time at home. However, some cats also enjoy frequent interaction, so it's important to consider their emotional and physical stimulation needs.

b) Pet size and available space:

The size of the pet is another crucial factor. The home space should be sufficient for the pet to move around comfortably.

- Small spaces: If you live in an apartment, it might be more appropriate to adopt a small dog or a cat that can better adapt to confined spaces. Small breeds tend to require less space and are usually easier to manage in urban areas.

- Home with a yard: If you have a large yard or access to outdoor areas, you might consider larger dog breeds that need room to run and play.

c) Expectations about the emotional relationship:

Different types of pets offer different types of emotional relationships. It's important for prospective owners to ask themselves what kind of emotional bond they want.

- Independent pets vs. pets that seek constant companionship: Some pets, like cats, are known to be more independent and require less constant attention, while dogs, especially certain breeds, seek human companionship almost all the time. Determining what type of emotional relationship, you want is key to making the right choice.

2. The Responsible Adoption Process

Objective: Explain the steps to adopt responsibly, ensuring that the chosen pet comes from a proper and ethical environment.

Responsible adoption goes beyond simply choosing a pet. This section educates future owners about the importance of adopting from shelters or organizations that promote animal welfare and how the adoption process can impact both the pet's and the owner's life.

a) Adopting from shelters or rescues:

Adopting from a shelter or rescue organization is an ethical and responsible option, as these organizations are dedicated to rescuing animals abandoned or mistreated.

- Advantages of adopting from a shelter: Shelters usually care for animals until they find a home, providing veterinary care, socialization, and sometimes basic training. Additionally, adopting from a shelter helps alleviate the issue of animal overpopulation.

- Assessing the pet's emotional needs: Many animals in shelters have gone through traumatic experiences. It's important to consider that some pets may require more patience and emotional support as they adjust to their new home.

b) Selection process and requirements:

Explain the steps involved in the responsible adoption process, such as visiting the shelter, interviewing the staff, and potential evaluations some shelters conduct to ensure the adoptive home is suitable for the pet.

- Shelter visits: Prospective owners should plan visits to the shelter to meet the animals in person. Observing how they interact with different pets and seeking guidance from shelter staff is essential for making a good choice.

- Adoption requirements: Many shelters have requirements that include background checks, signing adoption agreements, and being open to follow-up visits to ensure the pet is in a proper environment.

c) International adoption: special considerations:

In some cases, future owners may opt to adopt a pet from another country. This section explains the additional challenges and considerations, such as health requirements, vaccinations, and transportation, that need to be taken into account before choosing this option.

3. Preparing for the Pet's Arrival

Objective: Help future owners prepare their home and environment to receive the pet, ensuring a smooth and safe transition.

Before bringing a new pet home, it's essential to prepare the environment to ensure it is safe, comfortable, and conducive to the pet's adjustment.

a) Physical space: creating safe zones:

Pets need a space where they feel safe and comfortable when they arrive at their new home.

- Resting area: Providing a comfortable place for the pet to rest, such as a dog bed or a cozy corner for cats, is key to helping them feel at ease. Newly adopted pets may feel overwhelmed by their new environment, so having a quiet zone is essential.

- Home safety: Ensuring the home is free of dangerous objects (electrical cords, toxic products, small items that could be ingested) is vital for the pet's safety.

b) Basic supplies: what you'll need:

Having the right supplies ready before the pet arrives makes the transition smoother.

- Food and water: Buying the appropriate food for the pet's age and needs is essential, as well as ensuring clean food and water bowls are available.

- Toys and enrichment items: Providing toys and items that stimulate the pet's mind will help keep them busy and prevent boredom. Interactive toys like balls or scratchers are great for dogs and cats, respectively.

- Walking and care accessories: Make sure you have leashes, harnesses, and grooming products (brushes, suitable shampoo) based on the needs of your new pet.

c) Preparing the family for the arrival:

It's important that all family members are aligned and prepared to welcome the new pet.

- Roles and responsibilities: Establishing who will be responsible for tasks like walking, feeding, or cleaning helps create a routine for the pet. This is especially important in families with children, as it teaches them responsibility and how to care for a living being.

- How to introduce the pet to children: If there are children in the house, it's important to teach them how to interact with the pet respectfully and calmly. Guidelines can be provided on how children should approach, pet, and play with the new pet to avoid overwhelming or scaring the animal.

4. The First Days at Home: Building Trust from the Start

Objective: Provide practical advice for the pet's first days of adjustment, helping establish mutual trust and comfort.

The first days are crucial for building trust between the new owner and the pet. This is a period when the pet may feel insecure or frightened, and the initial focus should be on creating a calm and supportive environment.

a) Gradual adaptation to the new environment:

It's important to allow the pet to explore their new home at their own pace. Some pets may feel curious right away, while others may be timider and need more time to adjust.

- Give the pet space: Let the pet explore the home without pressure. Don't force interaction immediately. Give them time to feel comfortable in their new environment.

- Supervision and safety: During the first days, it's important to closely supervise the pet to avoid them feeling disoriented or getting into trouble. For cats, a helpful technique is to temporarily confine them to one room before allowing them to explore the entire home.

b) Initial routines and setting boundaries:

From day one, establishing routines is essential to help the pet adapt to their new home.

- Regular feeding and schedules: Establishing regular feeding times and walks helps the pet feel secure and understand what to expect.

- Training and boundaries: While the first days are mainly for creating a relaxed environment, it's helpful to start setting some clear boundaries, such as where the pet can or cannot go, or which behaviors are acceptable. Positive reinforcement training from the beginning is key.

c) Patience and empathy: keys to success:

It's important to remember that the pet is experiencing a major change and may take time to adjust. Patience and empathy are essential during this period.

- Realistic expectations: Some animals adjust more quickly than others. It's important to have realistic expectations and give the pet time to feel safe and comfortable.

- Building trust: The first days may be challenging, but with patience, affection, and consistency, you will lay the foundation for a long-term trust-based relationship.

Conclusion of the Chapter: The Beginning of a New Life Together

This chapter concludes with a reflection on the powerful beginning that adopting a pet represents. The arrival of a new furry companion marks the start of a life filled with shared moments, love, and mutual learning. By preparing the environment and welcoming the pet with patience and empathy, owners not only ensure a smooth transition but also begin the journey toward a deep and meaningful emotional relationship.

Chapter 9: Overcoming the Loss of a Pet: Grief and Emotional Healing

Chapter Summary: The loss of a pet is one of the hardest moments for any owner. This chapter addresses grief and the emotional process that follows the death of a beloved animal companion. Through a blend of reflections on grief, practical advice for coping with the pain, and suggestions on how to honor the memory of the pet, this chapter offers comfort to those experiencing sadness and loss, helping readers to heal emotionally and find meaningful ways to move forward.

1. Understanding Grief for a Pet: The Emotional Stages

Objective: Explain the different stages of grief and how they can manifest after losing a pet, offering validation and emotional support for those going through this experience.

Grief over a pet is as valid as any other loss, and it's important for owners to understand that it's normal to feel profound sadness when such a special companion is gone. This section explores the stages of grief, helping readers recognize their emotions and feel supported throughout the process.

a) The Stages of Grief: What to Expect Emotionally

Grief is an individual process that manifests in different ways, but it often includes some common emotional stages, similar to what is experienced after the loss of a loved one.

- Denial: The initial stage of shock and denial, where it is difficult to accept the reality of the loss. Many people may feel that their pet's death is unreal or temporary and may continue to expect to hear their pet's footsteps at home.

- Anger: It is common to feel anger or frustration after a pet's death, whether directed at the situation, oneself (for not having done more), or even at the veterinarian. This anger is a manifestation of deep pain.
- Bargaining: In this stage, people often think about the "what ifs" or "if only I had..." trying to understand or reverse the fact of the loss.
- Depression: Once the reality of the loss sets in, deep sadness can dominate. The owner may feel an emotional void, a sense of loneliness, and ongoing sorrow.
- Acceptance: Over time, while the pain never fully disappears, people reach a place of acceptance. The pet will always be remembered, but the grief becomes more manageable, and healing can begin.

b) Grief Has No "Right Time"

Everyone deals with loss differently, and there is no set timeline for grief. Some people may heal faster, while others need more time. This section emphasizes that grief should not be rushed or avoided, and that everyone should allow themselves to feel the pain at their own pace.

c) Comparing Pet Loss to Other Losses

Sometimes people may feel they shouldn't be so sad over losing a pet because society doesn't always recognize this type of grief as legitimate. However, the bond between humans and animals is deep, and losing a pet can be as devastating as losing a human loved one. Validating this experience helps readers accept their pain and find comfort.

2. Different Ways to Cope with Grief

Objective: Provide practical strategies and tools for coping with grief after the loss of a pet, helping readers navigate the healing process.

Grief is a deeply personal process, and there is no one-size-fits-all approach. This section offers a variety of strategies that pet owners can use to deal with sadness and find solace.

a) Emotional Expression Through Memory

One of the healthiest ways to cope with grief is to allow yourself to remember the pet in a positive way. Talking about good times, looking at photos, and sharing stories can help keep the pet's memory alive while going through the grieving process.

- Creating a Memory Journal: Suggesting that readers write a journal with stories, anecdotes, or special details about their pet. This activity can be very therapeutic, allowing them to relive happy moments and express their sadness safely.

b) Emotional Support from Friends and Family

Talking about the pain with friends, family, or members of the community can be a great source of comfort. There is no need to go through grief alone, and sharing feelings with those who also loved the pet or understand the pain is very important.

- Support Groups: There are specific support groups for pet loss, where people can share their experiences and receive emotional support from others who have gone through similar situations. These groups, both online and in-person, provide a safe environment to talk about the loss without judgment.

c) Therapy or Grief Counseling

For some people, the loss of a pet can trigger deep emotions or even exacerbate pre-existing emotional issues like depression or anxiety. In these cases, seeking the help of a professional, such as a grief counselor, can be very helpful for processing emotions in a healthy way.

- Cognitive Behavioral Therapy (CBT): This technique can help owners reframe negative or intrusive thoughts about the loss and focus on healthier ways of dealing with pain.

3. Supporting Children Through Pet Loss

Objective: Provide readers with strategies to help children cope with the loss of a pet, adjusting the process according to the child's age and understanding.

For children, the death of a pet may be their first significant experience of loss. This section offers practical advice for parents to guide their children through the grieving process in a healthy and comprehensible way.

a) Explaining Death to Children

It's important to be honest with children about the death of a pet, using language they can understand. Avoiding confusing terms like "went to sleep" or "went to heaven" can help children better understand what happened and process their emotions.

- Adapting the Explanation by Age: Younger children may not fully grasp the permanence of death, so it's helpful to repeat the explanation in a simple and calm manner. Older children may have deeper questions about life and death, and it's important to be prepared to address these questions honestly.

b) Allowing Children to Express Their Emotions

Encouraging children to talk about how they feel and express their sadness is essential in helping them process grief. Children often need permission to cry and be sad, as they may feel they need to "be strong" for the adults who are also grieving.

- Creating Symbolic Rituals: Involving children in symbolic activities to remember the pet can be a powerful way to help them process grief. Planting a tree in memory of the pet or drawing pictures of happy moments shared are examples of how children can express their love and sadness.

c) The Long-Term Impact of Grief on Children

Grief can have lasting effects on children, and it's important for parents to watch for any changes in behavior or mood over time. Some children may need additional support to overcome the loss, and in more severe cases, it may be helpful to consult with a child therapist.

4. Honoring the Memory of Your Pet

Objective: Offer ideas and suggestions on how owners can honor the memory of their deceased pet, helping them find ways to keep their pet's emotional legacy alive.

Honoring the memory of a pet is a positive way to channel pain and remember the happy times shared. This section suggests creative and personal ways to keep the pet's legacy alive.

a) Creating a Memorial Space at Home

Some owners find comfort in creating a small altar or space dedicated to their pet, with photos, favorite toys, or even an urn with their ashes. This space can serve as a constant reminder of the love shared and offer a place for reflection.

- Photo Album or Video: Creating a photo album or even a video of the best moments is another beautiful way to remember the good times. It is a cathartic activity that allows one to focus on the positive legacy of the pet.

b) Symbolic Memorial Rituals

Performing a ritual or ceremony to say goodbye to the pet is a powerful way to process the loss. Some people choose to bury the pet in a special place or scatter their ashes in a location with emotional significance.

- Planting a Tree or Flower in Their Honor: Planting a tree, shrub, or flower can serve as a living and lasting tribute to the pet's life. Every time you see the tree grow or the flower bloom, it will be a symbolic reminder of your companion.

c) Performing Charitable Actions in Their Memory

Another meaningful way to honor the memory of a pet is to perform acts of kindness in their name. Donating to an animal shelter, adopting another pet in need, or even volunteering at a shelter are ways to keep the spirit of your pet alive.

Conclusion of the Chapter: The Legacy of Love That Endures

The chapter will conclude with a reflection on the emotional legacy that pets leave in our lives. Though the pain of losing them is profound, the lessons of love, loyalty, and companionship they gave us are gifts that stay with us forever. By honoring their memory and allowing ourselves to feel the pain of grief, we also open the door to healing and remembering our beloved pets with lasting gratitude and love.

Chapter 10: Pets and Families: Integration and Healthy Relationships

Chapter Summary: The relationship between a pet and the members of a family can be one of the most meaningful that exists. Pets are not just companions; they also influence family dynamics, teaching values like empathy, responsibility, and unconditional love. This chapter explores how to successfully integrate a pet into the family unit, ensuring that both adults and children, as well as any existing pets, interact in a healthy way. Practical advice is offered on building a solid relationship and how pets can foster emotional well-being and family unity.

1. Introducing a New Pet into the Family

Objective: Provide practical guidance on how to introduce a new pet into the home, especially when there are already other family members or pets in the household.

Bringing a new pet into the home, whether into a family with children or one with existing pets, is a delicate process. This section offers a step-by-step guide to ensure that the transition is as smooth as possible.

a) Preparing the Family for the Pet's Arrival

Before the pet arrives, it's essential to prepare the family emotionally and logistically for the new addition. This involves setting clear expectations and creating a welcoming environment.

- Family Communication: It's important that all family members are involved in the decision to adopt a new pet. Having discussions about what caring for a pet entails, responsibilities, and house rules will help establish a solid foundation. Make sure everyone understands what it means to commit to caring for a living being in the long term.

- Setting Clear Expectations and Boundaries: It's helpful to define which areas of the house will be accessible to the new pet and what behaviors are expected from both the pet and family members. For example, will the pet have access to beds or only certain rooms? Setting boundaries early on will make the pet's adaptation easier and reduce potential tensions.

b) Introducing the Pet to the Family: Key Steps

The moment of introduction is crucial in determining how the relationship between the new pet and family members will develop. First impressions can make a big difference in the emotional bond that forms.

- Allow a Gradual Introduction: Don't force immediate interactions; give the pet space to feel secure and not overwhelmed by its new surroundings. Let the pet explore its new home at its own pace, and allow it to approach family members when it feels comfortable.

- Create a Calm Environment: It's important that the house remains calm during the pet's arrival. Avoid loud noises or large gatherings in the first few days, as the pet will need time to adapt to its new home without feeling stressed.

- Observing Behavior: During initial interactions, observe the pet's body language and that of the family members. The pet may show signs of anxiety or stress, such as licking its lips, excessive panting, or keeping its tail low. It's important to give space and not pressure the pet to interact too much.

2. Children and Pets: Teaching Responsibility and Empathy

Objective: Show how the relationship between children and pets can be a powerful tool to teach responsibility, empathy, and respect for living beings.

One of the greatest joys for many children is growing up with a pet. Through this relationship, children can learn valuable skills and values that will serve them throughout their lives.

a) Assigning Age-Appropriate Responsibilities

Involving children in pet care from the start is an excellent way to teach them responsibility. Depending on the age, they can be assigned simple or more complex tasks.

- For Younger Children (Ages 3-6): Younger children can participate in simple tasks, such as helping fill the water bowl or picking up the pet's toys. While they aren't old enough to take on major responsibilities, these small tasks help them feel useful and teach them about daily care.

- Older Children (Ages 7-12): As children grow, they can take on more important tasks, such as feeding the pet, cleaning its bedding area, or helping with walks. These responsibilities teach them consistency and the commitment required to care for another being.

- Teenagers: Teens can take a more active role in pet care, such as handling veterinary visits, training the pet, or even learning to recognize signs of physical or emotional discomfort in the animal.

b) Fostering Empathy Toward Animals

One of the most valuable lessons pets can teach children is empathy. By interacting with a pet, children learn to interpret the body language and emotional needs of another living being.

- Interpreting Pet Body Language: Teaching children to observe and interpret their pet's signals, such as whether it's happy, tired, or stressed, helps them better understand the emotional world of animals. For example, teaching them that a dog with ears back or hiding may be scared or anxious.

- Games That Encourage Respect and Care: Supervised games that promote positive interactions, such as playing fetch or using interactive toys with cats, are great ways to strengthen the bond between children and pets.

c) Supervision and Safety During Interactions

While pets are part of the family, it's essential that children, especially younger ones, are always supervised when interacting with them. Even the friendliest pet can feel uncomfortable or stressed, and it's important to teach children to respect the pet's space and signals.

- Setting Interaction Limits: Teaching children not to disturb the pet while it's eating, sleeping, or resting is crucial to maintaining a safe and respectful relationship. Children should learn that the pet also needs its own space and time to relax.

3. Managing Dynamics Between Multiple Pets

Objective: Provide strategies for integrating a new pet into a home where there are already other pets, avoiding conflicts and fostering harmony.

Introducing a new pet into a home with existing animals can be challenging, but with proper planning, it's possible to create a positive living environment.

a) Careful Introductions Between Pets

Introductions between the new pet and the resident pets should be done carefully, ensuring that both feel safe and not threatened.

- Gradual and Supervised Introduction: The introduction should be gradual, allowing the pets to smell and interact through a barrier (such as a door or gate) before seeing each other face-to-face. This approach reduces stress and anxiety, especially for more territorial animals.

- Controlled Interactions: The first interactions should be short and closely supervised. Owners should be attentive to any signs of discomfort or aggression, such as growling, raised fur, or tense postures. If either pet shows signs of stress, it's important to give them more time before attempting another introduction.

b) Managing Territory and Resources

One of the main causes of conflict between pets is competition for resources such as food, toys, or resting spaces.

- Separate Areas for Each Pet: Initially, each pet should have its own designated space for eating, resting, and playing so they don't feel forced to compete for resources. This helps reduce tension during the first few weeks of cohabitation.

- Sharing Over Time: As the pets become more accustomed to each other, shared playtime or joint activities can be introduced, always under supervision to ensure peaceful coexistence.

c) Positive Reinforcement to Foster Harmony

Using positive reinforcement, such as treats or praise when the pets behave well together, is an excellent way to encourage peaceful interactions. Rewarding calm and respectful behaviors between pets teaches them to associate the other's presence with positive experiences.

4. Pets as Emotional Support for Family Members

Objective: Explore how pets can provide emotional support to family members, from children to adults, and how this strengthens family bonds as a whole.

Pets can offer significant emotional support, providing comfort, companionship, and unconditional love to all family members. This section focuses on how pets can play a key role in the emotional health of the family.

a) Pets and Managing Family Stress

The simple act of petting a pet can reduce cortisol levels (the stress hormone) and increase the release of oxytocin, the hormone associated with well-being. For many, time spent with their pet is a natural way to relax and disconnect from daily worries.

- Support During Crisis Moments: Pets can provide invaluable comfort during tough times, such as the loss of a loved one, financial difficulties, or work-related stress. Their constant and affectionate presence helps ease tension and offers a safe emotional haven.

b) How Pets Strengthen Family Unity

Caring for a pet is a shared responsibility that can strengthen the sense of unity within the family. From walks to playtime or simply being together with the pet, these activities create moments of connection and shared joy.

- Family Rituals with Pets: Having family rituals that include the pet, such as weekend walks together or planning group playtime, reinforces the bond between family members and the pet.

c) Pets as Emotional Support for Individuals with Special Needs

Pets can also provide crucial emotional support to family members facing mental or physical health challenges. For example, emotional support animals and therapy dogs provide companionship and emotional stability to people with anxiety disorders, depression, or autism spectrum disorders.

Epilogue: The Bond That Transforms Us

Throughout these pages, we have explored the deep and meaningful bond that unites humans with their pets. From the emotional power they bring us to the daily routines that strengthen that connection, this book has offered a comprehensive look at how our pets not only enrich our lives but also teach us important lessons about love, empathy, and resilience.

Pets aren't just companions who fill our days with joy; they are silent teachers who show us how to live in the present, appreciate the small moments, and become more human. Each chapter has shown how this bond can nurture both our emotional health and that of our furry friends, creating a mutual support relationship that transcends time.

Thank you for sharing this journey. May the love you feel for your pet continue to flourish, and may that bond remain a source of joy and strength throughout the years.

Disclaimer

This book is intended for informational purposes only and is based on research, personal experiences, and general recommendations regarding the well-being of pets and their owners. The information contained within these pages should not be considered a substitute for professional guidance from veterinarians, therapists, or animal behavior specialists. If your pet experiences health or behavioral issues, it is essential to seek the help of a qualified professional who can provide an appropriate diagnosis and treatment based on your pet's specific needs.

The author and publishers do not assume any responsibility for damages or losses that may arise from the use or misuse of the information provided in this book. Every pet is unique, and their individual circumstances may require specific solutions.

Don't miss out!

Visit the website below and you can sign up to receive emails whenever Gonzalo Estrada publishes a new book. There's no charge and no obligation.

https://books2read.com/r/B-A-OZBBB-SLHCF

BOOKS 2 READ

Connecting independent readers to independent writers.

Also by Gonzalo Estrada

Self Healing
Visualiza tu Éxito
Cultivando Líderes
Transforma tu Mentalidad en Tiempo Récord: Afirmaciones Poderosas
para Alcanzar tus Metas
Semillas de Cambio
Cómo convertir TikTok en una máquina de hacer dinero
Cómo hacer dinero con Pinterest
Cómo hacer un ensayo
Cómo Pedir un Aumento de Sueldo
Currículo Poderoso
Entrenamiento sin Violencia
Entrevista Laboral
Gana Dinero con X (Twitter)
Ganar Masa Muscular
Volver a Empezar; el arte de reinventarse
Analiza Resuelve Ejecuta
Aromatherapy, The natural path to your pet´s well being
Holistic Feeding
The ABC of Educating Your Pet
The Art of Cosmic Connection
The Art of Feng Shui applied to your Pets
From Scarcity to Abundance
The English Bulldog in The Family
The French Bulldog

Therapeutic Massages for Pets
Pets and Crystal Therapy
The Maltese Bichon
Transform Your Problems into Opportunities
Esto ya Cambió
Cómo crear Prompts de forma correcta.
Mejora tu productividad personal
Ecommerce Catálogo Extendido
Finding your way back
Strong by Habit
Jack at Dawn
HAZLO: La Metodología Definitiva para Formar Hábitos Exitosos y
Transformar tu Vida
La bicicleta de Mónica
The Invisible Bond